Get Ready To Race

story by Arthur Roulo

illustrations by
Barbara Nascimbeni

HARCOURT BRACE & COMPANY

Orlando   Atlanta   Austin   Boston   San Francisco   Chicago   Dallas   New York
Toronto   London

Have you ever been in a race?
You'll do your best if you know
how to get ready.

It helps to practice with a friend.
It's more fun, too.

Eating well gives you energy.
That will help you run fast.

Sleep well the night before.
Rest is good for you.

Stretching gets you ready.
Your legs will be ready to run.

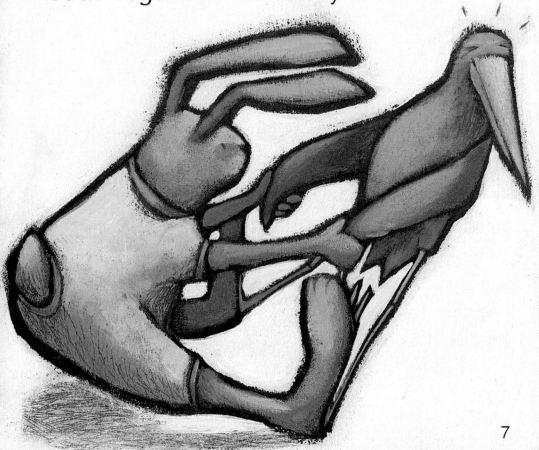

Wear clothes and shoes that feel good.

Remember to breathe.
It helps you relax.

If your body hurts,
STOP and rest.
Running is hard work.

Be proud of yourself.
Believe in yourself.

If you are ready to race,
you'll be ready to race to
the finish line.